The Wisteria Tea House
(A rhyming bedtime tale of a princess and her tea house)

Written by Audrey R Jones

This work was originally registered with the U.S. Copyright Office under the title "The Wisteria Tea House."

Copyright © 2025 by Audrey Jones.

This book is intended for entertainment and educational purposes only. While the story may contain themes of bravery, adventure, and imagination, parents and guardians are encouraged to read along with young children and use their discretion in guiding discussions. No part of this book is meant to replace professional advice, cultural consultation, or historical fact. All rights reserved by the author and publisher.

All rights reserved. No part of this book may be reproduced, stored in a retrieval system, or transmitted in any form or by any means—electronic, mechanical, photocopying, recording, or otherwise—without the prior written permission of the copyright owner, except in the case of brief quotations embodied in critical reviews or articles.

First edition
Illustration design by Nafeesa Arshad

Printed in the United States of America
ISBN 978-1-80623-790-6 (hardcover edition)
ISBN 978-1-80623-789-0 (paperback edition)
ISBN 978-1-80623-788-3 (ebook edition)
Library of Congress Control Number: 2025922512

Published by Audrey R. Jones, in association with The Author's Point

For My Youngest Daughter

The Wisteria Tea House
(A rhyming bedtime tale of a princess and her tea house)

Written by Audrey R Jones

Illustrated by Nafeesa Arshad

In a garden where flowers grew wild and free,
lived a girl in a crown, as proud as could be.

Her name was Sarabear, with curls full of spring,
she danced through the garden as if it was a king's ring.

She wore fancy clothes and dresses with flair, and sparkled with joy from her crown to her hair.

She twirled on the stones and waved to the trees.
Her voice floated gently on the soft morning breeze.

Her mama would watch from the garden gate, smiling and thinking, "it's time to create…"

"Mama?" asked Sarabear, "What are you doing?"
"I'm building a secret," she said, gently shooing.

She painted and hammered, tied bows in the breeze, and hung purple blooms from the Wisteria trees.

She whispered to petals and measured each beam, creating a place from a sweet, quiet dream.

The tea house she built was cozy and sweet, with cushions and cups and a tiny wood seat.

Its windows were lace, the floor soft with mats, and corners held stories and pink paper hats.

Right next to the roof, a birdhouse stood tall, and soon a small sparrow made it her hall.

"Tweet-tweet!" sang the bird from morning till noon, a melody floating in perfect toon.

Sarabear came running in glitter and gold,
"this is the prettiest tea house to hold!"

She poured make-believe tea with a curtsy and grin, and invited the sparrow and butterflies in.

She read to her dolls, each crowned as a queen, and sketched little menus in crayons of green.

Each afternoon when the sun started low,
the Wisteria whispered and began to glow.

Mama brought biscuits, warm honey and cheer, and Sarabear would giggle, "So glad you are here!"

She told little stories with sparkle and light,
of castles and dragons and stars in the night.

And even as Sarabear grew taller each day, the tea house still called her to laugh and to play.

For a crown can be quiet, and magic can stay, in a house made of love and dreams never fray.

Under that tree, with Wisteria in bloom,
Sarabear still visits her fairytale room.

A Special Note

Every child deserves a space where imagination can bloom, a place built not of bricks, but of love, wonder , and play. Sarahbear's Tea House is more than a story of crowns, blossoms, and pretends tea. It is about the bond between parent and child, the gift of creativity, and the magic of making turning ordinary moments into extraordinary ones. As Sarabear grows, the tea house remains, a reminder that childhood dreams never truly leave us. They transform, they follow us, and they become the quiet corners of our hearts where joy still lives. This story invites us, as adults, to remember that crowns can be simple, magic can be lasting, and love, when given freely, builds a home for wonder that time cannot take away.

www.ingramcontent.com/pod-product-compliance
Lightning Source LLC
Chambersburg PA
CBHW041124070526
44584CB00003B/273